THE SMALL BIG BOOK OF DOGS!

Written and illustrated by

RANSOM ROGERS

The Small Big Book of Dogs

Text copyright © 2017 Ransom Rogers
Illustrations copyright © 2017 Ransom Rogers

Editor: Ruth Valorie Catabijan
Layout Artist: Giona Mae Reyes

First Edition: October 2017

ISBN: 978-971-625-372-6

How to Order
Purchase individual copies from: https://shopee.ph/st.matthewspublishing

Copies are also available at special rates in bulk orders. Contact the publisher through the details below.

St. Matthew's Publishing Corporation
First RVC Building, 92 Anonas Cor. K-6th Streets, East Kamias, Quezon City
(02) 8426-5611 || inquiry@stmatthews.ph
www.stmatthews.ph

To Ging and Noli, my strength, my pillars, my virtue.

FOREWORD

Ahoy, dear reader! Fellow dog-lover here.

Growing up, I have had a couple of dogs who have been my companions during lazy afternoons in the province, where you really had nothing to do but sit and stare at dust collecting in windowsills. They were my best buddies when I was sick, and some of my best memories during my probinsya days included them—Patchie and Benjie—visiting parks, beaches, and going to the market early in the morning.

I'm guessing you picked this book up because you—just like me 20 years ago—are planning on getting a dog as a pet, but don't know where to start. Well, look no further! This book has everything from choosing your fur buddy, to feeding them properly, to teaching them simple tricks (totally cool)!

All of these come with fun illustrations that can teach you, your mom, or your dad how to give your new dog the care and attention it needs to be happy and healthy.

The Small Big Book of Dogs, a book for young 'uns with big hearts!

Happy reading!

Toto Madayag
Creator of Libreng Komiks

TABLE OF CONTENTS

An Introduction to Dog Ownership
A message from Ransom Rogers

An Introduction to Dog Ownership

Welcome, new friend! It's with great pleasure that I welcome you to *The Small Big Book of Dogs*. I assure you that, one day, you'll look back and think of this as one of the best decisions of your life. Now, I will be your host, your guide, and your buddy in this endeavor: Ransom Rogers!

Caring for dogs is a commitment. There will be hard times, but in the end, the reward of a life-long friend and companion who will never leave you is more than worth it.

I've been a dog owner for years, and I've met, cared, and befriended many of them in my lifetime. It has always been my goal to give them a good, fulfilling life in the time we spend together.

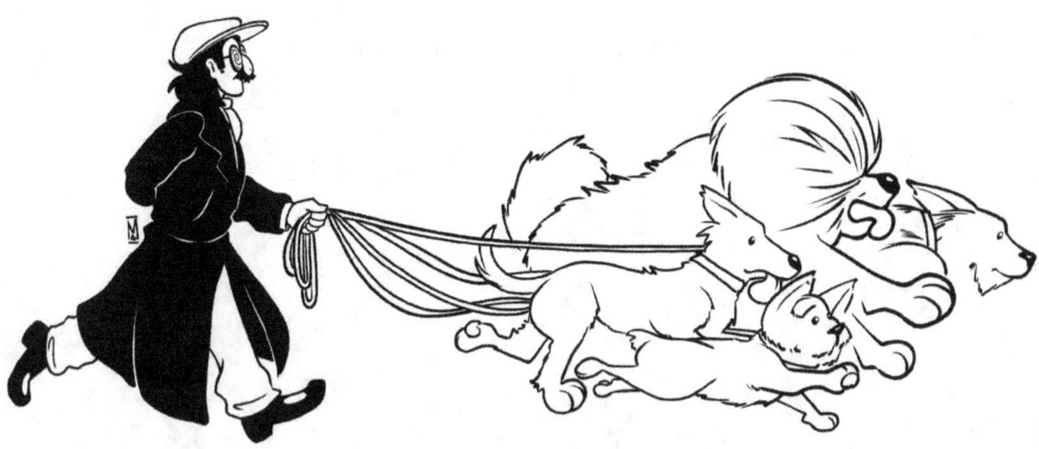

So, what does this book have to offer you?

First of all, we'll be going through the things you need to consider before you get a dog. We'll learn how to take care of them, both in terms of everyday care and when they're sick. Finally, we'll learn ways to have better fun with your dog, such as learning how to teach them tricks.

There will be a great deal of basic knowledge that will put you on the right track. That's what the "small" part of *The Small Big Book of Dogs* means, after all. It's small enough to fit in your pocket, but bursting at the seams with knowledge and know-how. It never hurts to supplement knowledge with more learning from outside sources, but this book is a good start!

Here we'll learn the very basics, from picking out a breed that suits your home and needs to feeding, simple tricks, grooming, and play. There are plenty of dogs out there that need a good home, and I want to give you a quick word of thanks for having an interest in giving one a new home.

You don't need to be a professional to be a good friend to your dog. Learn by doing, I say! And with that, I bid you luck, friend.

Yours truly,
Ransom Rogers

Chapter 1
The Many Different Kinds of Dogs
And which one is best for you!

"I Want a Puppy!"

Mr. Reyes is a hardworking father, so hardworking in fact, that he normally comes home to a sleeping daughter and a cold dinner. But on this particular evening, he finds a child running to him as soon as he steps out of his car.

"I want a puppy!" she exclaims. Leah looks up at her father, wide-eyed and giddy. Mr. Reyes hugs her tight and raises her up. "Good evening, anak," he tells her. "What's this about?"

Mrs. Reyes is standing at the front door, smiling, with her arms crossed. "She's seen a film about a boy and his dog, and now she wants one, too," she explains.

Mr. Reyes sets Leah down on a soft patch of grass. "A dog is a huge responsibility! It won't be like having a toy, you see," he tells her.

"I know," she replies. "I have to feed him, and walk him, and play with him, too!"

"And you'll be cleaning after him, too!" says Mrs. Reyes. "It'll be like having your own baby!" she chuckles.

Leah looks at her mom and shouts, "Then, I'll be the best mummy, you'll see!"

"I'm sure you will be, anak!" says Mr. Reyes as he pulls his suitcase from the boot of his car. "Tell you what," he says, "let's all head inside and turn in for the night. We can talk about getting you a puppy in the morning."

Leah's face turns sour, and she stomps back inside in a huff right past her mother. "She's been awfully excited with the idea all evening," says Mrs. Reyes. "I'm afraid she'll be in a bit of a mood if we don't do something."

Mr. Reyes thinks for a while, and then he smiles. "I've got it!" he says. "I have the perfect thing."

Mr. Reyes hurries to bring his things in, get changed, and eat his cold dinner of nilagang baka. He ventures to the garage and looks through the old boxes and cupboards, Mrs. Reyes tailing behind.

"What are you doing, love?" she asks him.

Mr. Reyes walks unperturbed to an old dusty box lying in the farthest corner. He opens it, pulls out an old book, and shows it to his wife. "This," he tells Mrs. Reyes as he hands it to her.

"The Small Big Book of Dogs?" she asks.

"Yes!" says Mr. Reyes. "My father bought it for me when I was young, even though we never got a dog ourselves." Mrs. Reyes follows him as he heads to Leah's room.

He raps on her bedroom door, and soon, the sleepy child opens it to greet him. "I've got a surprise for you, Leah, my darling!" he tells her. Leah's eyes beam up.

"What is it, daddy?" Leah asks.

"I know you're excited about getting a dog," Mr. Reyes explains. "But before we let you have one, you need to know a lot more about them!"

Dogs by Size: Yappers, Doggos, and Woofers

We can easily classify most dog breeds into three types: Small, Medium, and Large.

Small

Ex.: Beagles, French Bulldogs, Yorkshire Terriers, Dachshunds, Miniature Snauzers, Pembroke Welsh Corgis, Cavalier King Charles Spaniel, Shih Tzus, etc.

Small-sized dogs, or "Yappers," are some of the most adorable little creatures to grace your home! So-named for their high-pitched barks, these dogs are fit for small living accommodations like apartments or bungalows. These little tapping paws will be very comfortable with a family of humans in a cozy home.

Did you know?

Some small-sized dogs are what we call "Toy" dogs, and they are a much smaller variety with more energy relative to their size.

Medium

Ex.: Labrador Retrievers, Bulldogs, Poodles, Boxers, Siberian Huskies, Border Collies, Weimaraners, English Springer Spaniels, Shiba Inus, etc.

Medium-sized dogs, or "Doggos," are the types of dogs that best come to mind when thinking of a family dog. Strong enough to endure athletic activities like fetch or running, these loyal friends are also thought of as good-natured and protective. Some of them, like the Labrador Retriever and the Belgian Malinois, are employed by the police and the military to make sure we're safe from any threats. Especially good for a nuclear family, they're not too expensive to maintain and care for.

Large

Ex.: German Shepherds, Golden Retrievers, Rottweilers, Doberman Pinschers, Collies, Akitas, Bloodhounds, Alaskan Malamutes, Dalmatians, etc.

Large-breed dogs or "Woofers," so-named for their deep, imposing barks, are huge dogs that require a lot of care and responsibility. They are big and some may require a large lawn in your home to frolic in. Nevertheless, a woofer raised right is a gentle giant, and can always be relied upon to be a proud member of your family!

> **Note:**
>
> They also eat a whole lot so it might be worth thinking about the cost of keeping them fed!

Breeds for Beginners

Not every dog is fit for a first-time owner. A lot of them require surprising amounts of care not normally available at your average pet store. We'll be listing a few recommended breeds here, but if there are other breeds that take your interest, or these dogs aren't available for adoption at your local shelter, don't be afraid to ask the custodians or veterinarians in charge for what they think might be appropriate.

Bichon Frise

A small-sized dog with curly hair, they're also relatively easy to maintain. They need a lot more grooming than most common dogs, but it should be fairly easy to learn how to groom them.

Papillon

Light, energetic, and easy-going, these small, long-haired dogs are very playful and enjoy time with their adopting family. A big personality in a small package, these yappers are great for any occasion.

Golden Retriever

A very reliable breed, they're an honest type that is perfect for families. They're low-maintenance and are easy to train.

Greyhound

Surprisingly docile for their size and build, greyhounds feel more at home lazing around with their owner. But, if you wish to challenge them, they can work well with athletic owners as the Greyhound can run with the best of them.

Labrador Retriever

A close cousin to the Golden Retriever, these dogs are similar to them, if only slightly more difficult to train. That said, they're a good companion as they'll follow you absolutely anywhere.

Poodle

Poodles come in different sizes. Regardless of the size of the dog you get, they make for very cozy and accommodating companions. They're easy to train and to get along with. The only drawback is the regular grooming. However, they shed a surprisingly low amount of fur!

Doctor's Tips

Some of you reading this may have what we call allergies. These are bad reactions our body has to certain things that can manifest as rashes, shortness of breath, or itchiness. These may include food, medicine, or animals. Always ask your vet or shelter staff if the dog you want is of a hypoallergenic breed if you believe you may have allergies. It's also best to visit a doctor called an allergist before you consider taking a dog home. Your life may depend on it!

Chapter 2
Getting a Dog
All you need to know to get yourself ready!

Leah's New Book

Every day after school, it became like clockwork for Leah to pull out the book Mr. Reyes gave her and read it on the bus ride home. She would pore over it, page after page, again and again, until she could almost recite the letters and the words by heart. It was almost a game to her, but the excitement gave it purpose.

Mr. Reyes promised Leah that he would bring her to the shelter to adopt a dog at the end of the week if she promised to read the book from cover to cover. Leah was determined. She would be the best mummy of all!

Now, Leah had a friend on the bus. His name was Nathan, and he already owned a dog. That made him her newest best friend. She would ask him all sorts of questions.

"What do you give them when they're hungry?"

"Do they like belly rubs or back rubs more?"

"How do you make them play fetch?"

"Can they talk if you teach them?"

Nathan was not a boy to be cowed, oh no. He knew the answers to all of these, of course. At least, that's what he liked to tell himself.

"It's simple, you see," Nathan told the doe-eyed Leah. "It all comes naturally!

Leah sat there, waiting for Nathan to talk more about the deep and exciting secrets of dog ownership. He often tells her, "If you can't get it first try, then that means you're not meant to have a dog! It's that easy." Leah felt slightly upset.

"What if I don't get it on the first try?" she asked herself. "Does that mean I'm a bad owner?" Leah puzzled over this. It would be very sad if she failed, but if she just studied harder, maybe it'll all work out! She had a secret weapon after all, she thought, as she clutched her father's old book tight to her chest.

"Just a few more sleeps," she muttered. "I haven't even thought of a name yet!"

Visiting Your Local Shelter

It may be tempting to go to a breeder to take home your favorite breed, but a lot of dog enthusiasts and experts are encouraging new dog owners to instead head to their local animal shelter.

A lot of dogs have been abandoned for one reason or another. While there are centers set up to take them, the dogs they take in aren't meant to live there forever. That's why they wait for eager people to help them find these dogs their forever-homes. It is ultimately your choice if you want to fully care for a dog wherever he or she may have come from.

Buying the Essentials

Before you go out and adopt a dog, it might be helpful to consider a few things to have before you need them.

Collar and Leash

Your dog is going to need a lot of exercise, and nothing helps better than a standard leash and a collar. Get a good quality collar. Some owners prefer ones made of leather to make sure the collars are as comfortable as possible for their dogs.

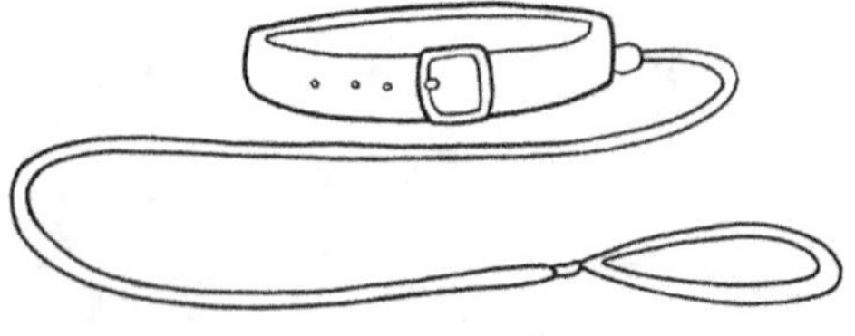

Tag

No matter how well your dog gets treated at home, it is possible that they might get out of the house. A tag comes in handy in such situations. You can get a custom-made tag to include your pet's name and your contact details. This way, your little buddy can make it back home safe and sound if someone happens to find them.

Dog Crate

During your buddy's first few days in his or her new home, you'll want to keep them in a crate. Usually, it's made of plastic or stainless steel, and strong enough to weather some wear and tear. It is useful for housetraining your pet or transporting them from place to place over long distances like trips to the **vet.**

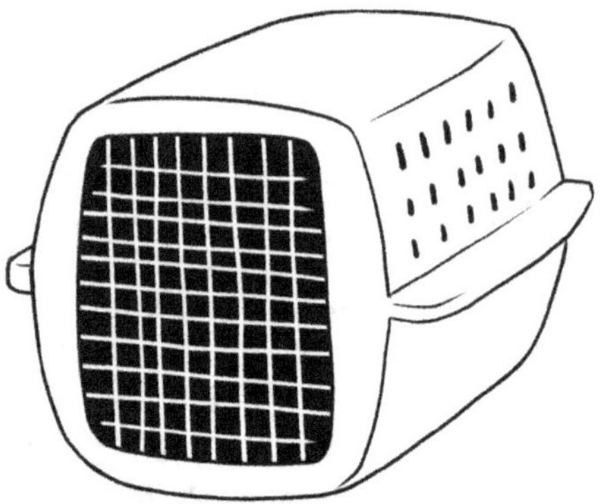

Food and Water Bowls

Your dog is going to need something to eat and drink from! Some owners prefer colorful plastic bowls. Others would rather use the more durable ones made of stainless steel.

Dog Bed or Dog House

If you intend to keep your dog indoors, a bed is a necessary addition to your home, especially if you or anyone in your home wouldn't like a dog taking up a bed usually meant for people.

If your dog is expected to grow bigger, consider buying a large bed to accommodate their size as they age.

Some owners take the covering of the dog bed and rub it on their skin to help puppies with separation anxiety to accept the bed as an extension of their owners' presence.

For outdoor dogs, always give them adequate shelter from the weather with a well-built doghouse. Some people commonly use cages to house their dogs but it is highly discouraged. They are uncomfortable for dogs and are not supposed to be used as a long-term home for them.

Grooming Supplies

You'll want a good set of grooming tools for your dog. This includes bath essentials like shampoos, towels, water supply, and others. Combs, cotton balls (for the ears), scissors, nail clippers, doggy toothbrushes and toothpastes are necessary, too. For the grooming of any non-short hair breed, your vet might recommend you take home a bristle brush and a hair dryer.

Food and Treats

Bring home some high-quality dog food from the pet store. Ask your veterinarian what type of food works for your dog. There are helpful labels on most of the different brands that tell you what breed that specific bag of dog food is for. You'll also want some extra-tasty treats, particularly if you intend to train your dog.

Different Types of Staple Dog Foods:

1. *Kibble (Dry Dog Food)* – Common and commercially available, this type of food is often sold in bulk. It doesn't need to be refrigerated and can be stored for a long time. Hard and crunchy, it even helps your dog maintain their dental hygiene.

2. *Canned (Moist Dog Food)* – Perfectly suited for dogs with problems in chewing due to age or disease, canned dog food is usually more expensive.

Treats for Your Dog

Sometimes, you'll be giving your dog a few treats as a reward or as a snack. These aren't like staple foods, meaning you can't expect these to fill your dog's stomach. It's alright to give your dogs some treats once in a while, but be careful to avoid spoiling them with it or you run the risk of your dog saying no to their regular meals.

Store-bought treats come in different types—from jerky to biscuits and everything in-between. They can be very expensive though. However, one of the things we have to keep in mind is that many of the treats available to your dog can be found in your kitchen.

Human Food for Dogs:

1. Peanut Butter – A doggie favorite. Avoid brands that are "low in fat" or "sugar-free," as these can have artificial sweeteners that are toxic to dogs.

2. Cooked Chicken – Cut them in strips as a quick, healthy treat. Use only the meat and avoid giving your dog the bones.

3. Baby Carrots – Good for your dog's dental hygiene on top of being very healthy.

If there are human food items that are good for dogs, there are also some that you have to absolutely avoid giving to your dog.

Human Food Items You Should Avoid Giving to Your Dog:

1. Almonds
2. Chocolate
3. Cinnamon
4. Garlic
5. Onion
6. Ice Cream
7. Macadamia
8. Avocado
9. Citrus
10. Raw/Uncooked Meat
11. Salty Snacks
12. Cooked Chicken Bone

Toys

Last, but not the least, buy some toys for your dog to play with! Puppies' teeth hurt a lot when their teeth start growing out, a process called **teething**. In addition to using them for play, toys can be handy for avoiding damages to your furniture.

Toys can come in all shapes and sizes. They can be distinguished by their use: for the dog alone to use or for owners to use if they want to play with their dogs.

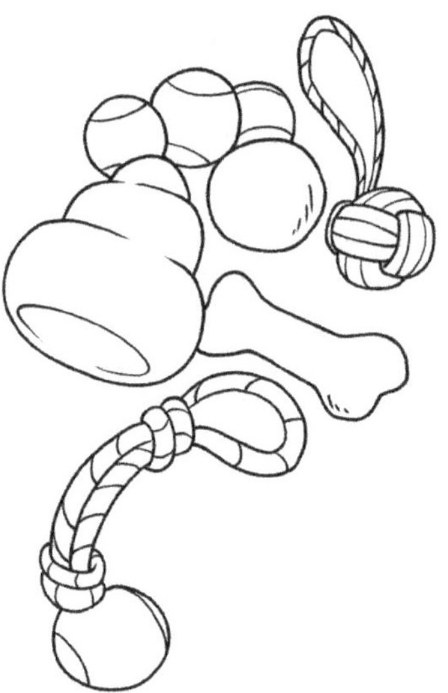

Soft, squishy rubber toys are perfect for a dog on their own, especially since it helps them deal with teething. Make sure that it fits in their mouth. A bundled rope paracord is sometimes used for owner-dog play. They usually have two handles that let you hold it on one end while your dog can grip the other.

> **Tip!** These are some of the essentials for common breeds, so if you're going to be taking home a more exotic breed, it might be helpful to ask a veterinarian what else you'd need for them.

The Handy-Dandy Checklist

Feel free to scribble on the sides if you have other things you think you'll need, but we'll do our best to cover the essentials here. We'll also be providing a separate checklist for the grooming supplies as they can get a bit confusing because there's a lot you'll need.

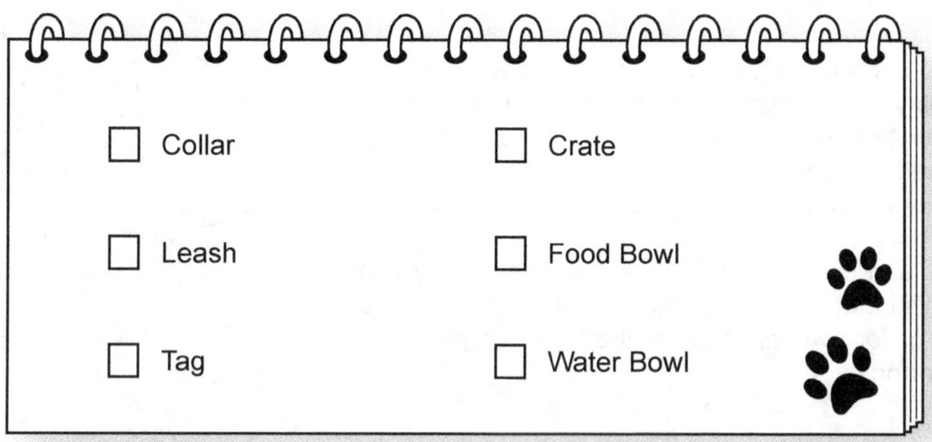

Grooming Supplies

- ☐ Dog Shampoo
- ☐ Dog Conditioner
- ☐ Dog Tower
- ☐ Comb
- ☐ Cotton Balls
- ☐ Scissors

- ☐ Nail Clippers
- ☐ Dog Toothbrush
- ☐ Dog Toothpaste
- ☐ Bristle Brush
- ☐ Hair Dryer

Puppy-Proofing Your Home

It's important to note that your dog, especially if they're still a young pup, is similar in many ways to a newborn human. It will be curious. It will try to chew everything, and without supervision. It might get hurt with the various things around the house we take for granted. A house must be puppy-proofed to avoid any unnecessary trouble.

Puppy Enclosure

If there are certain areas of the house that you want to keep your dog out of for any reason, it is wise to buy steel, collapsible enclosures that you can assemble anywhere. It will help fence off areas that might be dangerous for your puppy or might have items that could be damaged.

Electrical Sockets

Keep dogs away from electrical sockets. They might chew on the cords plugged there or hide them or tuck them away out of reach when not in use.

Child-proof Latches

Consult an adult on installing child-proof latches. These will help make your home safer by making it more difficult for your dog to access areas that normally contain materials that are dangerous to them. Your dog will eventually grow to learn which items they should and shouldn't touch, but as they are still a pup, it's better to err on the side of caution.

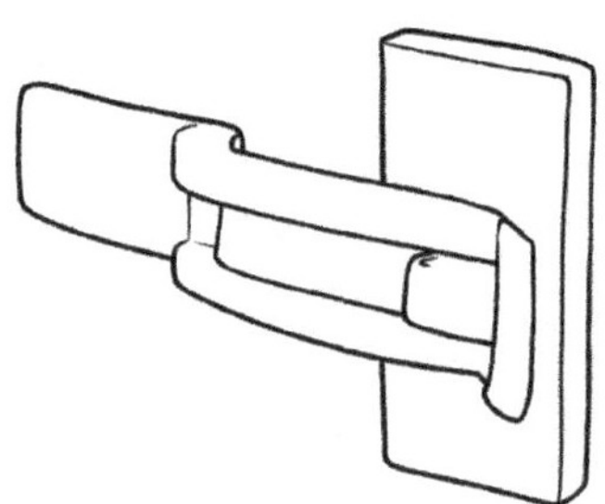

Tip! As much as possible tidy up your home often to keep your dog away from hazards or dirt.

You'll also want to be paying careful attention to your puppy, instructing them what they can or cannot approach. This is a very crucial time in their development, and the most adorable. Be sure to take good care of your new puppy around the house!

Making Room in the Budget

Having a dog is a huge responsibility. You'll be taking in a living being that needs food, rest, sleep, and a warm place to stay. All of these are things we normally consider for ourselves, so a new dog should also be treated as a family member. That means that if you or your family is struggling to make ends meet as you are now, consider a better time in the future when you can get a new dog. If you're not in control of your family budget, ask your parents or guardian if you can afford to set aside a portion for a potential pet adoption.

You also have to consider the non-monetary needs of caring for a dog. You have to understand that a dog will not always understand what you want from it, and having one around requires a great deal of patience.

Dogs are smart, but they will need a lot of help to understand what you want to tell them. Taking care of them is a commitment, both in terms of the time and money you're willing to spend on them.

Again, make sure you have the following before getting a dog:

- ✓ Time
- ✓ Patience
- ✓ Money

Chapter 3
Housetraining Your New Roommate
House rules for everyone.

Welcome, Brownie!

Leah was having trouble sleeping. She was imagining what kind of dog she'd get, as there were certainly lots and lots of them in her father's *Small Big Book of Dogs*.

"It's time to sleep, anak. We don't want you all sleepy when we pick up your new friend!" said Mr. Reyes.

"I'm ready, dad!" Leah shouted. "I read up like you told me to, I know all there is to know about having a dog! Ask me anything, I'm sure I'll know the answer!"

Mr. Reyes smiled. "I'm sure you did a good job, Leah. You're a very bright girl," he said. He stayed with Leah, stroking her hair until she fell asleep.

The next day, Leah was up early ahead of Mr. and Mrs. Reyes. When Mr. and Mrs. Reyes woke up, they found their daughter already bathed, dressed, and clutching her bag. They had breakfast, and soon left for the shelter.

The shelter was about an hour's drive from the Reyeses. When they arrived, they were greeted at the door by a portly man in half-rim glasses named Maurice, and greeted him good morning. They all went inside, where they met a young woman. Her name was Ann, she told them.

"And, who will be picking out a dog to take home?" Ann asked the two. Leah's arm shot up into the air.

Ann brought them to the kennels, where they kept the dogs that were up for adoption. It was a narrow corridor, with cage doors on either side. There was a knee-high wall covering each enclosure, and Leah had to tiptoe just to see the other side.

In the first enclosure was a big, old dog. It had a brown muzzle and a coat of black fur that was already greying. Leah felt sad for the old dog. It looked lonely.

"There are others here," she said. "This one is old and taking care of him might be too much for a first-time pet owner."

The second enclosure held a litter of little fawn-colored pugs. They immediately ran to her and started yapping through the bars.

"Oh, they're so rowdy together! I'm not so sure you'd want such an energetic pack." Ann yelled.

"Can't we take just one of them?" asked Mrs. Reyes.

"You could," said Ann. "But we found that they get very sad and lonely if they're away from their brothers and sisters. It might be too much work, considering they're all newborns."

Mrs. Reyes turned to Leah, but the eager young girl had already gone ahead. She was looking into an enclosure at the end of the hall, where a small, golden pup was peering over to look at her in turn.

"Ah, sad story about that one." Ann said. "Youngest and only survivor of a litter of four. The mother died as well soon after giving birth, leaving the poor thing on its own."

"What's his name?" Leah asked.

"Well, the old owner said he would have named him Brownie," answered Ann. "But if you choose to adopt him, you can give him any name you want."

"If he already has a name, maybe he'd like it to still be the same?" asked Leah. Mrs. Reyes looked at Ann and nodded.

Mr. Reyes and Maurice were outside the kennel room when Leah came out, clutching a young pup In her arms.

"Daddy, meet Brownie!"

Teething, Biting, and Barking

A few things to note when handling your puppy: they can display some seemingly aggressive behavior that might make you think like they're upset or angry. Most of the time, however, especially with younger puppies, this type of behavior is usually associated with growing pains and can be curbed with the right treatment.

Teething

If you decided to bring home a puppy of only a few weeks, chances are their teeth might still be coming in. This is what you call teething.

Teething pains will lead them to try and relieve it by way of exercising their gums. This usually translates to chewing on the nearest surface they can grasp with their mouth, and often times it might be your mother's favorite furniture.

Note:
Teething doesn't always equate to hunger, so try not to overfeed your dog.

There's nothing you can really do as the pain they are experiencing will come regardless. To avoid chewing on furniture and other important items, you can direct your dog to something they are allowed to chew like dog toys.

Dog toys come in all shapes and sizes. Some are even flavored to encourage dogs to chew on them instead of anything else.

Biting

There can be a number of reasons your dog develops a biting behavior. Experts agree that biting usually comes about because of things like fear arising from meeting something or someone new, or pain from any part of their body. Maternal or mommy dogs that just gave birth can be eager to bite, for  an understandable reason, as are dogs who tend to be possessive of their food or toys.

Biting is often playful more than it is harmful. Some owners are uncomfortable or otherwise scared of having their dog's teeth so close to their bodies. You may check to see if this behavior persists for more than a few days. If your dog starts biting you for no reason for an extended period of time, bring them to your local veterinarian for a checkup as it may reveal some illnesses that only show up when properly tested.

Barking

Dogs are naturally inclined to bark at things that might seem strange to them. They do it to protect themselves and the people they love, usually having it mean "go away!" Some things that dogs are exposed to on a regular basis lose this strangeness to them and the dog itself feels less inclined to bark at it. 

In general, it's a good idea to ignore your dog to let them know that you disapprove of their behavior. Avoid shouting at your dog as this makes them believe you're only barking with them.

Leaving and Coming Home to Your Dog

Dogs are pack animals. That means they feel most at ease with their "pack mates," which is, in this case, their human family.

Whenever dogs are left alone, they feel terrible and abandoned. This feeling is called separation anxiety. This makes it difficult to keep your dog from getting excited every time you come home. At worst, your dog may pee on itself in an act of submission and excitement.

It's best for you to remain calm before entering the home, and taking your dog outside to let it pee or poop. As with most unwanted behaviors like those, it's always best to stay collected and to avoid shouting at your dog.

Getting Along with Other Dogs

If you have other dogs at home that are waiting to greet their new brother or sister, here are a few tips to keep in mind.

It will be helpful to introduce them to each other in a guided fashion. The "home" dog will naturally be defensive of its territory. Any new pets at home might be seen as a threat by the "home" dog. One way around this is to introduce both dogs to each other somewhere neutral, and once they're more comfortable with one another, they can be brought to your house.

Let dogs interact and establish boundaries with play fights by themselves. This is usually encouraged as it allows the dogs to come to terms with each other much better than if a human were to intervene. However, it will be best to keep an eye on both dogs during their first few days together to avoid any violent contact.

Shared Feeding

An important thing to note is that you'll have to teach your dogs to respect each other when it comes to mealtime. They won't always understand the concept of sharing or giving way, so it's your responsibility to teach them how. Here are a few tips I'd like to share.

1. Buy a new set of bowls for your new dog. Your "home" dog might consider its bowls as part of its territory, and won't be willing to share.
2. Keep your new dog in its crate when feeding them. This enables them to have a safe environment to eat in without having to worry about the "home" dog stealing their food.
3. In the case of multiple dogs, some owners recommend keeping all of them in their crates when feeding time comes around. This helps form discipline when it comes to mealtimes and helps avoid any unnecessary conflict.

> **Tip!** For other kinds of pets, it generally follows the same principles. Keep them separate until calm, introduce them together in a controlled environment, and always have a way to restrain them in case a fight breaks out.

Chapter 4
Poop! Poop Everywhere!
And a bit of wee, too.

Brownie Made a Mess!

"The doctor said that the puppy might get a bit stressed when we bring him home," said Mrs. Reyes.

"Does that mean he's worried?" asked Leah. She turned to Brownie sitting in a dog crate next to her on the backseat of the family car. "You don't have to be worried, Brownie! We'll play lots and lots and have plenty of fun, you'll see!"

"Nothing like that, dear," said Mr. Reyes. "I'm sure Brownie is very excited to be in a loving home, but right now he just doesn't know us too well so he's a bit scared."

"That, and he might not poo immediately," said Mrs. Reyes.

"Why is that important?" asked Leah, her head tilted.

"Because we'll have to make sure to teach Brownie where to poo," answered Mr. Reyes. "Dogs aren't as easy to teach as people are to use the proper bathroom, so we'll have to guide him when the time comes."

Leah nodded her head and turned to Brownie. "You'll be a good boy and not make a mess, right?" Brownie stuck his tongue out and tried to lick Leah's face through the bars. She took it as a "yes."

Hours passed and just as Mrs. Reyes said, the puppy was still awfully bashful and rarely came out of his crate. They'd made a small enclosure with some collapsible fences that Mr. Reyes bought from the hardware store on the way home. They littered Brownie's living area with a few soft cotton pads and some newspapers. Dinnertime came and Brownie still hadn't made a poo.

"What time did you give him food and water?" asked Mrs. Reyes.

"As soon as we came home!" answered Leah. "But he still hasn't touched it."

"Maybe he just needs a bit of company to get settled in," said Mr. Reyes.

"But, I've been with him since this morning!" said Leah. "I want to stay with him until he does!"

"Alright then," said Mr. Reyes. "But you can only stay up until it's time for bed."

As soon as dinner and chores were done, she changed into her pajamas and set off for the living room with The Small Big Book of Dogs in hand.

"Don't worry, little Brownie!" Leah shifted in her father's favorite armchair until she was snug. "I'll be here with you!"

Not too long after though, Leah quickly fell asleep.

The next morning, Leah awoke to a very foul smell. She looked over to Brownie's enclosure and found the food bowl empty, and right in the middle, Brownie had parted the pads and the newspapers to reveal a bit of the carpet, upon which nestled a small pile of his poo.

Going to the Bathroom

There will be poo. A lot of it, in fact. Caring for a dog means you'll be picking up after it often. It can get easier with a bit of commitment and dedication.

Dogs have a bunch of reasons for leaving their poo, also known as droppings, where they do. Sometimes it's to mark their territory, other times it's an attention-seeking move. Whatever the case, with or without cause, they will be pooping and peeing a lot. The key is to learn how to manage it and to effectively address any issues as they come up through careful monitoring.

"The Business" in the Great Outdoors

Ah, the great outdoors. It's the perfect place to teach your dog where to leave his droppings as it's a lot easier to clean up and you can use a rake and an old dustpan to dispose of the mess. You also don't have to worry about any traces of poop on the dirt or on the grass. Nature will take care of the rest.

The problem with teaching dogs to poo outdoors is that dogs don't easily understand our instructions. We cannot simply tell them to go and poo outside. We have to teach them how to do it.

Guiding Your Dog to a Proper Place to Poop.

1. Feed your dog while keeping it inside its crate.
2. Once your dog is done, carefully lead it outside. Use treats or a leash, but never force your dog. It has to be taught to come out on its own.
3. If your dog begins to poop or pee inside its crate before you've led it out, use a loud noise like a clap to get their attention and say "Ah-ah!" or "No!"
4. When your dog is outside and at a suitable spot for pooping, walk it around in circles and keep quiet. Be patient here.
5. Once your dog begins to go, whisper the phrase or command you wish to use when you want it to poop later on. My favorite command would be, "Do the do-do!"
6. Praise your dog for a job well done. Offer it some treats if you have any.

"The Business" Indoors

It is very rare for an owner to want a dog doing their business indoors, but there are products that can help you out.

Dogs generally prefer to do their business outside, in the open air, and on a nice patch of grass. If this sort of environment is unavailable where you live, you can choose to purchase an indoor dog potty and a pee pad.

An indoor dog potty works like a cat's litter box. Like a litter box, it is a small plastic tray with a surface where dogs can poop. Unlike a litter box, however, it has a sheet with fake grass on top meant to catch the poop instead of sandy litter.

Training is almost exactly the same as described on page 40, the only difference here being where you dictate the desired pooping spot for your dog.

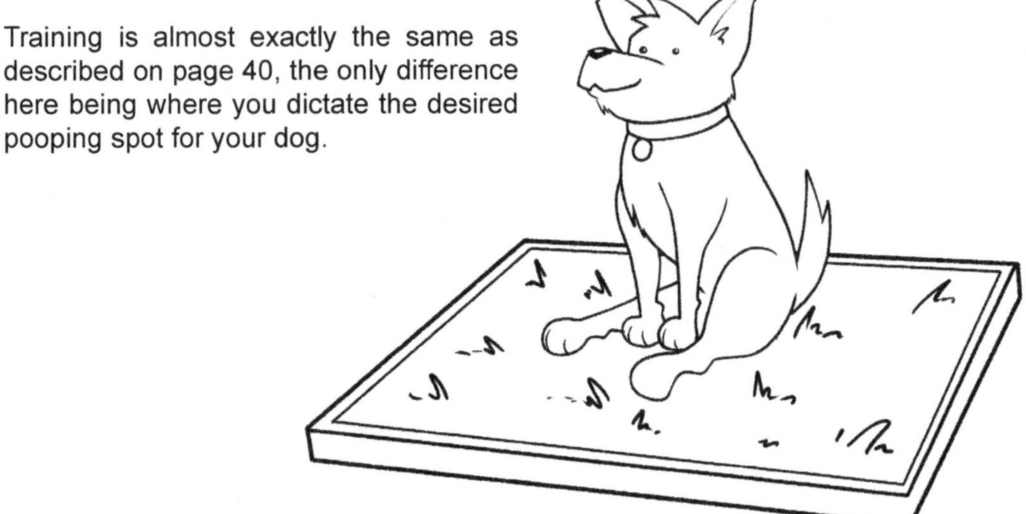

Helpful Tools

Have some tools ready to make sure that you can easily and safely handle any waste material.

Pee Pads

When first teaching your dog to pee in proper places, it helps to use pee pads. Ideally, your dog's pee pad is there to teach them to pee on command. It is going to be a bit expensive if treated as a permanent solution.

Cardboard Strips

Useful for picking up your dog's "accidents" off of solid floors. You can throw them out with the poop.

Carpet Cleaner

This is for when you have to clean up carpets or other fabric surfaces. Ask your parents or guardians for help when using chemicals.

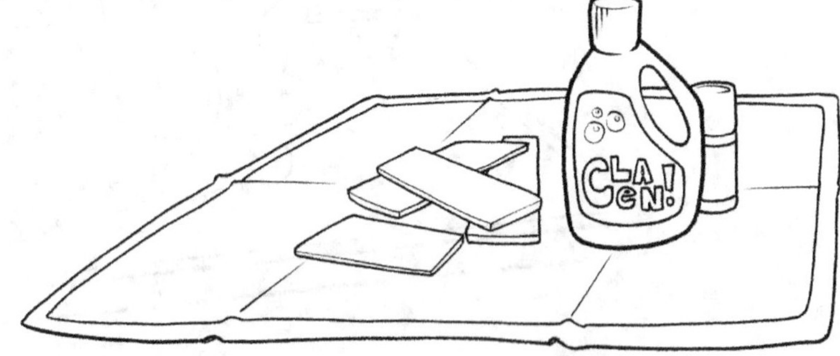

Chapter 5
Help, Doctor!
I think I broke my dog.

Brownie Doesn't Look Too Well...

Every morning in the Reyes household, just as the Reyeses would stir and wake, Brownie would hop from his bed and rush to greet them. He'd scratch at Leah's door until she got up and let him in, then he'd run circles around her before pawing at her legs.

Leah would carry Brownie down to the kitchen where Mr. Reyes has his morning coffee and Mrs. Reyes would be cooking a nice, healthy breakfast. This morning, it was bacon and eggs with a side of carrot and cucumber sticks. Leah started a habit of preparing Brownie's food and setting it by the breakfast table. "So, he doesn't get lonely eating by himself!" she'd tell her parents. Brownie was slowly becoming a part of the Reyes' family routine, and soon, the family itself.

One day, Leah woke to a quiet morning instead of hearing Brownie's tender paws scratching at her door. Leah leapt off her bed and ran for Brownie's nook in the living room. Mr. and Mrs. Reyes were already there, huddling over Brownie's bed. When Leah entered the living room, she heard a familiar tap-tap-tapping as Brownie gingerly walked to her. He licked her hand lazily, then went back to bed.

"He doesn't look too well," said Mr. Reyes.

"Not too well at all," murmured Mrs. Reyes.

"What's wrong?" asked Leah.

"What's wrong?" asked Leah. "We don't know," Mr. Reyes answered. "But, hopefully he'll be good again once he's had some breakfast."

But, Brownie never touched his meal.

Mr. Reyes left for work, as usual, leaving Mrs. Reyes to care for Brownie as Leah herself went to school.

On the bus home, Leah sat next to Nathan. She asked him if his dog had ever been sick, or never ate his food. Nathan grinned.

"Then, it's just being a bad dog!" he shouted. "When my Max doesn't eat her meal, I throw it away and tell her she'd been a bad girl."

Leah didn't quite understand and asked why.

"Because she was being ungrateful! That's why she deserved to be punished," said Nathan.

It didn't sit right with Leah. Brownie couldn't have been ungrateful or angry. She played with him every day, fed him every day, and even practiced her singing around him. She wondered what she was doing wrong.

On the way home, Leah found her mother and father waiting outside the house, dressed up. Mr. Reyes was putting Brownie's dog crate in the back seat.

"What's going on?" Leah asked. "Why are you home so early, daddy?

"I took the rest of the day off so we could bring Brownie to the vet, anak. Hop on in and we'll have him checked soon," he answered.

Before Going to the Vet

There are different reasons you'll have to take your dog to the vet outside of its normal schedule for visits. Dogs can get sick differently from humans. There may be some things you have to look out for that you're not used to.
Here are some tips to keep in mind.

Transporting Your Dog

Smaller dogs can be kept in crates for ease of transport. Bigger dogs can be taken along with a leash. When loading your dog into a car, make sure that you have some windows open. A closed car can make your dog dizzy and nauseous. Tell your vet everything that you listed down. Any small detail might help. Always be observant with your dog when you suspect it is ill.

Take Notes

Keep notes on your dog's behavior. Any sudden changes such as a loss of appetite or a noticeable increase in aggression or irritability should be noted.

Look out for any physical changes. Irritated skin or patches that are losing fur are of interest. Swelling in certain parts, and growths like lumps and bumps should also be noted.

Signs to Look Out For: Fleas, Worms, and Other Nasties

At some point, your dog will get sick. This isn't necessarily your fault as it happens to most dogs. The important part is recognizing the symptoms when your furry friend needs your help.

Fleas

Fleas are nasty parasites that latch on to your dog's coat and feed off of them. They mostly affect dogs, but sometimes an infestation can occur and it can spread to other pets and even people if untreated.

In the case of fleas, you can always look out for small, black, bumpy dots with legs that cling to your dog's coat. They should be easy enough to spot if your dog has short fur. If you own a long-haired dog, and it gets infested with fleas, your vet might recommend shaving off your dog's hair.

An infected dog will display excessive scratching, licking, or biting at its own skin. In some cases, there might also be hair loss in certain spots. If your dog appears to have a flea infestation, it is best to take them to a vet. A vet will often treat it with flea-killing shampoo, a special medicated collar known as a flea collar, or medicine to be applied on your dog's coat.

Ticks

Ticks are the bigger cousins of fleas and they're much, much worse. They can carry diseases that may cause your dog to vomit often and act sick or disoriented.

In some cases, ticks might cause your dogs to become weak, increase its heart rate, or possibly become paralyzed.

Compared to fleas, ticks are larger and more visible. They might still be able to hide in a long-haired dogs fur, only to be discovered later as a small bump on the dog's skin.

It is best to remove a tick with the help of an adult, or leave them in for a vet to remove. Improper removal of a tick bare-handed can cause an even worse disease that can infect not just your dog but also you.

Intestinal Worms

Worms are a trickier sort. They hide inside the dogs' bodies, hurting them from the inside. A worm infection could cause vomiting, diarrhea, tiredness, a bloated stomach, weight loss, a dull coat, or actual worms to appear in their droppings. Another tell-tale sign is when a dog scoots, or rubs its butt on the floor. A visit to the vet is always necessary here.

As a more complicated parasite, worms can range from harmless to life-threatening. Vets will first examine what kind of worms are present. They might use blood tests, x-rays, and other sorts of medical exams to determine the severity of the worms' effects on dogs. Often, your dog will only require a certain type of medicine that vets will inject into your dog's skin to solve this parasite problem.

Heartworms

Dogs infested with heartworms need long-term care. Treatment is very expensive, but necessary. Over the course of a few months, your vet will treat your dog by giving them special medicine. This will help prevent heartworms from growing and kill any that are already inside. After that, your dog will have to recover from the effects. Your vet will monitor your dog's progress for a few months to make sure they're healthy. A visit to the vet will be followed by a series of medical exams to determine the severity of the worms' effects on your dog. Often, the doctor will only prescribe some medicine, but in some rare cases, surgery might be necessary.

Preventive Measures

Just like with human babies, there are several health concerns you must consider when getting your dog especially if it is a young puppy. In this chapter, we'll discuss the various preventive measures that ensure a healthy life for your dog.

Neutering

Neutering a dog is something all responsible dog owners should do. It helps to curb any unwanted aggression. Neutering also helps you control your dog from having too many puppies. For male dogs, it's called castration, and for female dogs, it's called spaying. In general, they both mean that the doctor will use surgery to make their sexual organs nonfunctional. It helps prevent certain types of illnesses from manifesting.

According to the American Kennel Club, most veterinarians recommend it done to dogs at any point past eight weeks of age. A neutered dog will also be a lot less aggressive towards other dogs of the same sex.

Vaccination

Vaccination, however, is a very important part of your dog's health. Vaccinating dogs keeps them healthy and protected from parasites, bacteria, and viruses that could otherwise cause great harm to both them and possibly you. Your vet should be able to provide you with a schedule for vaccination, and some of them even have their own handy-dandy checklist so you can always keep track!

Some of the most essential vaccinations help deal with the following:

1. **Rabies** – an infectious disease caused by a virus called the lyssavirus. It can be very deadly to both dogs and infected humans. It causes dogs to have excessive aggression, hydrophobia (fear of water), and eventually, death.

2. **Leptospirosis** – bacteria that can cause heavy internal injuries such as bleeding from the lungs, meningitis, and kidney failure. Its complications can cause death.

3. **Kennel Cough** – an infection in dogs that can cause respiratory problems. It incubates for 7 days. After which symptoms such as dry cough, retching, sneezing, snorting, gagging, and vomiting appear.

4. **Heartworms** – *See page 50.*

5. **Corona Virus** – Also known as canine Coronavirus. It is a highly contagious intestinal disease that can cause vomiting and diarrhea.

6. **Parvovirus** – Canine parvovirus or CPV is a viral illness which can manifest in one of two ways: it can affect either a dog's intestinal system or its cardiac system.

7. **Distemper** – A serious viral infection with no known cure, and it affects the dog's respiratory, urogenital, gastrointestinal, and nervous systems.

So, don't delay! Visit your local **veterinarian and get your dog treated!**

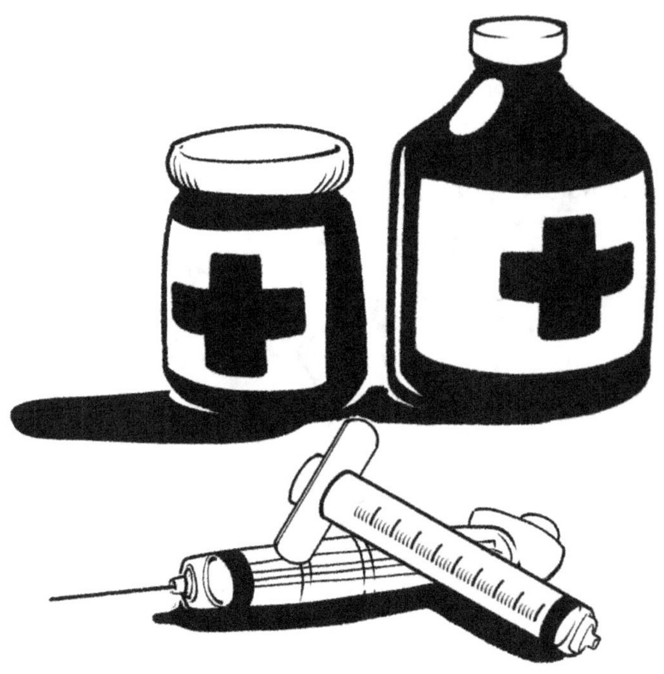

Post-treatment Needs

Even if you have your parents or guardians around when you take your dog to the vet for treatment, you still have to pay close attention to the doctor's instructions. Oftentimes, the problem doesn't end with a visit, even if most of it was already taken care of.

Medical treatment can often leave your dog vulnerable to more illnesses or injury, so listen closely to the doctor's post-treatment needs. A few of these may include the need for a cone around your dog's neck to prevent them from biting at their body a call for no baths for a week for the pooch.

Take notes if you have to when you're talking to your dog's vet. Once you take your dog home, you're going to be the best chance they'll have at recovering.

Some items that you may have to use
at home for post-treatment care include:

1. Pet cones
2. Medicine droppers
3. Medicated soap

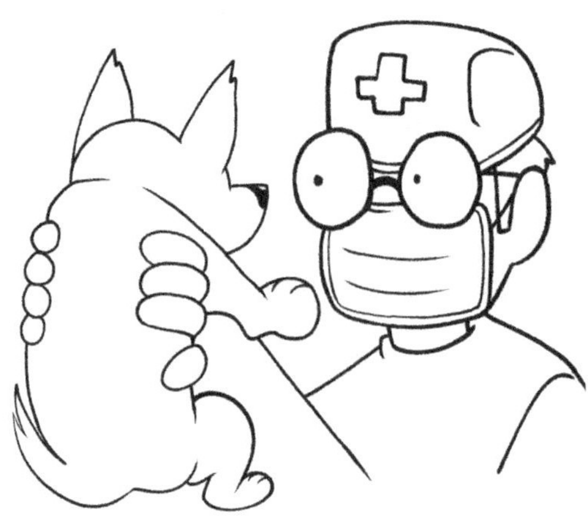

Health Check-ups

Human bodies get frailer as they grow older, but we see these changes more vividly in our canine companions. They grow up to live to about an eighth of a human lifespan which is about 13 years. Most of their years are spent near or with humans. If they're lucky, they will spend their lives with caring, loving humans. It's only right that, if we commit to take care of them, we try to give them the best experience they can have.

Part of this care involves regular check-ups for your dog as it gets older at ten years and above. Health issues tend to arise from genetic or external causes as dogs reach their double-digit ages. You might notice it from changes in their behavior, their energy levels, or just their appearance. It's our responsibility to make sure they're taken care of.

Common Symptoms of Illness in Dogs

Be mindful of your dog's health at all times. Happy, healthy dogs are usually chipper and cheerful, so any behavioral changes should be observed. Here are some of the most common signs to look out for.

1. Behavioral changes such as lethargy or irritability
2. Difficulty in walking, particularly when climbing stairs
3. Increase in peeing or pooping
4. Coughing and sneezing
5. Loud or audible breathing
6. Hair loss
7. Dry, itchy patches of exposed skin
8. Oversleeping
9. Growths in the skin such as lumps
10. Sudden changes in weight
11. Swollen tummy
12. Blood in poop

Please do not do this to your dog.
This is just a cartoon.

All Dogs Go to Heaven

At some point, we'll have to say goodbye to our furry friend. Someday, your dog will pass on. When that day comes, you may find it motionless in its bed. It's also possible that your dog might be too weak or too sick to get up anymore and a veterinarian will have to get involved to put your dog down.

Preparing for the End

When the time comes, you may choose whether to have your dog put down at home or at the vet's clinic. Ask your vet first if they allow home services. Putting down a dog is done with medicine injected into their bodies. You may be with your dog in its final moments if you choose to do so. They might spasm slightly. They may pee or poop themselves. Their eyes might not fully close. They might twitch as they take their final breath. This is normal. The important part is to be there for them.

Burial

Your dog may be buried in your home, though you must check with the local government if you are allowed to. Otherwise, there may be pet cemeteries you can bury your dog elsewhere. Your dog may also be cremated. Ask your veterinarian if they offer cremation services.

Goodbyes are hard. We just have to accept them, and to treasure our memories with our furry friends.

Every dog is special. The time they spend with us is a blessing from beginning to end. Even when the time comes that they're no longer with us, their memories will always stay.

Chapter 6
Sit! Stay! Don't Eat That!
What is in your mouth?!

New Dog, New Tricks

The Reyes family soon allowed Brownie to roam free around the house. They dismantled his enclosures and gave him toys to play with. However, to Mrs. Reyes' displeasure, Brownie had gained a taste for her woodworked stools and mahogany chairs.

"I won't stand for this anymore!" she yelled at Mr. Reyes.

"Darling, he's still a puppy. He's probably just exercising his teeth," he told her. They argued in the kitchen away from Leah. Leah looked over at Brownie, chewing away happily at one of Mr. Reyes' old shoes in the corner.

"There must be something we can do!" screamed Mrs. Reyes.

"I can try and train him!" said Leah.

Mr. Reyes chuckled. "You've never trained a dog before, Leah. Don't be silly," he jested. "We'll find a professional dog trainer and have him come around on the weekends."

"There's a part in the Big Book about making puppies stop chewing," said Leah. "It wouldn't hurt to try!"

"Alright, anak," said Mr. Reyes. "We trust you."

"But, we're still getting a trainer," quipped Mrs. Reyes. "At least for the harder stuff."

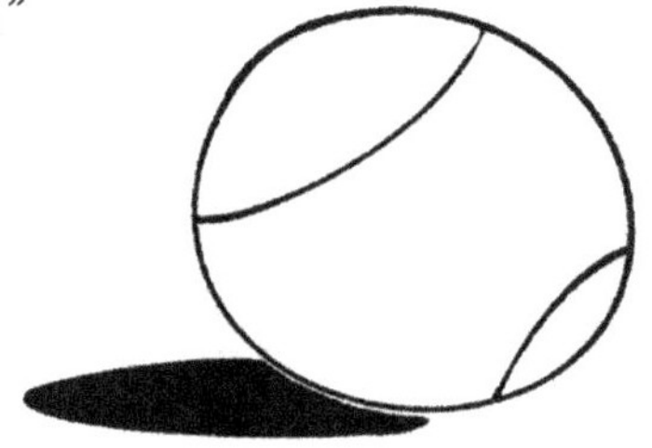

• • • • •

"You're getting a trainer?" asked Nathan on the bus home. Leah nodded.

"But, that's so lame!" the boy yelled. "All you really need is a stick!"

"To play fetch with?" pondered Leah.

"No, to hit them with when they do something bad!" giggled Nathan. He seemed pleased with himself as he mimed a motion that looked an awful lot like hitting a small animal. Leah was horrified.

Leah came home that afternoon to a young woman standing in their kitchen. She was talking to Leah's parents, patting Brownie on the head as he sat down by her feet.

"Leah," Mrs. Reyes started. "This is Bea. She'll be helping you train little Brownie."

"But, I've got the Big Book!" Leah protested. "I've got everything I need here!"

"I understand, anak," interjected Mr. Reyes. "But, it always helps to ask an expert."

"Don't worry, Leah!" squeaked Bea. "You, Brownie and I will be best friends!"

Teaching Basic Commands

At some point, you'll want to teach your dog what experts call "obedience commands." These are some of the few basic things you can teach your dog without too much difficulty or effort on your part. These commands only require some time, dedication, and a few treats to help.

Sit

1. Sit or kneel to match your dog's level.

2. Take a treat and put it up to its nose. Move your hand up slowly

3. Make sure that your dog's head is following the treat. As your hand goes further up and back, your dog should sit his butt down on the floor.

4. As soon as your dog sits down, give the treat to your dog while pairing it with the command, "Sit."

Come

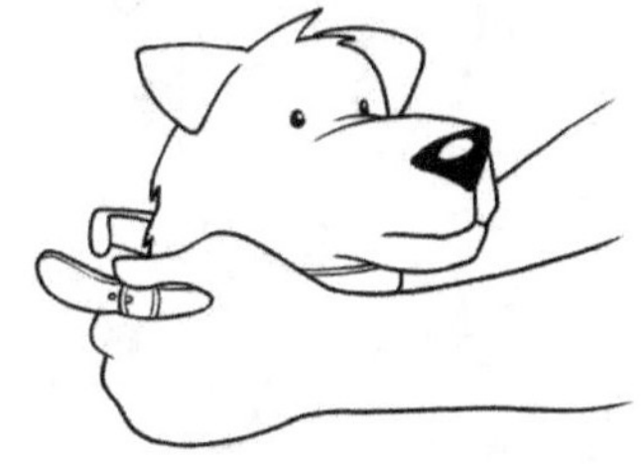

1. Attach your dog's leash on to its collar.

2. Take your dog for a light stroll around the house or in an open, but small space.

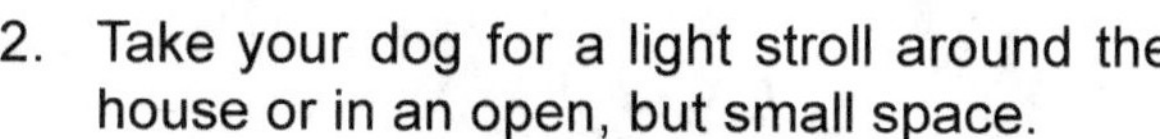

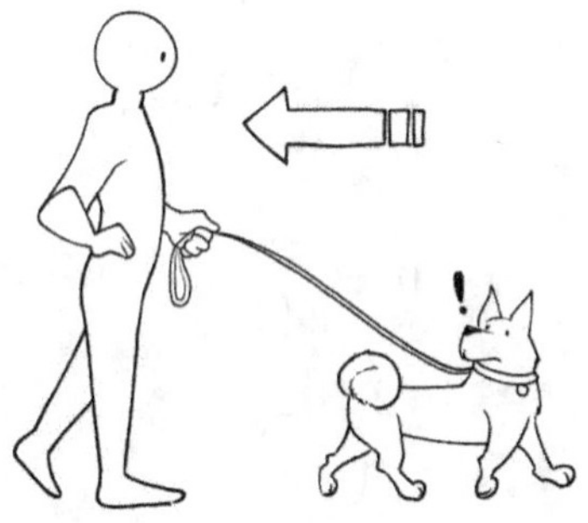

3. Once your dog is used to its leash, start walking backwards.

4. Your dog will whip around to follow you. As soon as he does, give him a solid praise. A "yes!" or "good boy!" will do.

5. Pair it with the command "come" just before you have him follow you. Offer a treat once he gets the hang of it.

Stay

1. Hold your dog with a leash and stand next to them.

2. With your palm out, hold your hand out to him as if telling him to stop, while loudly saying "stay."

3. Take a few steps forward without letting go of the leash.

4. Wait a few seconds before returning to your original position.

5. Offer a reward like a toy or a treat to your dog for a job well done.

Tips!

1. When training your dog to follow any command, say the command only once. This helps your dog understand that they must follow your command without waiting for you to repeat it.
2. When teaching the "Come" command, avoid using the command to call on a dog you wish to punish. He will start to disobey your command because he is scared of being punished.
3. Be consistent! Use the same words for the same command. This avoids the dog from being confused and will learn to obey you more effectively.

Chapter 7
Hit the Road, Jack!
But, be sure to be back by dinner.

Brownie Gets Anxious

"Good morning, Miss Bea," greeted Leah.

"No need for that," answered Bea. "You can just call me 'Bea!' Now, how have you two been?"

"Brownie and I have been doing well!" Leah declared. "He stops, and he sits, and he comes when I call him!"

Bea patted Leah on her head and stooped down to stroke Brownie's coat. "Have you taken him out for a walk yet?" she asked.

"Mum says he's too small to go outside yet," Leah blurted. "He might get caught in the wind!"

"Well, today's a lovely day," Bea reassured her. "This is just as good a day as any!"

They attached Brownie's leash onto his collar. Bea asked Leah to put on a hat and some good shoes. As soon as Leah came down the stairs, she found Bea and Brownie waiting by the door.

"Let's go!" said Bea.

Unfortunately, it wasn't the wind that kept them from going out for Brownie's first walk. Brownie simply refused to go out the door. Bea tried to coax him by laying down kibble, easing Brownie out of the house, step by step. They'd made it to about two feet past the Reyes' front door when Brownie refused to be pulled out any further.

"He seems a bit stubborn," Bea huffed. "That's okay. We've made good progress!"

"Really?" asked Leah. "We haven't even taken him out on his first walk yet."

"You can't force your dog if he doesn't want to," said Bea. "You have to remember that he's your friend. And, as his friend, you have to respect his decision."

"Does that mean he'll never want to go out?" Leah's lips quivered. "But, we treat him so well!"

"Oh, no." retorted Bea. "It's not your fault at all! Brownie will learn new things to do with you over time. He just has to conquer his own fears and, eventually, he'll trust you with anything."

Just then, a familiar voice startled them from behind.

"Having trouble with the mutt?"

It was Nathan, yanking his dog, Max, behind him. Her collar looked a bit too tight, Leah thought, as she noticed the folds of skin that wrapped around it.

"Just give it a good tug! She'll be following you right out!" he yelled from the sidewalk. Nathan walked on, dragging Max by the neck and disappearing past a corner.

"That boy doesn't know what he's talking about," quipped Bea. "And, his dog doesn't seem to be having a good time."

"You think so?" asked Leah.

"Yeah," Bea answered. "Do me a favor and don't listen to anything he says. He seems like an awful pet owner. We'll try again tomorrow, yeah?"

Leah nodded as they took Brownie back inside the house.

Your Dog's First Walk

Dogs that start their puppyhood indoors will not be too eager to get out of the house for the first walk. They will have to be coaxed with treats or otherwise calmly called to go out.

Always be patient with your dog. Often, they don't follow a certain instruction out of fear, uncertainty, or anxiety. Teach them to be more trusting of you by giving them constant reassurance and praise for a job well done.

Leashes: Regular, Retractable, and Slip Collars

There are many different types of leashes and collars for your dogs. Aside from the different materials available such as nylon and leather, there are also different types of collar and leash combos to use for different situations.

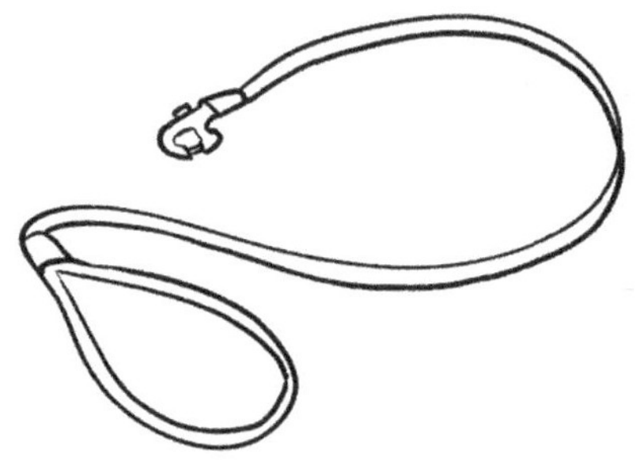

Regular/Simple Leash

A simple leash is just as it says: a piece of rope you use to hold on to your dog. Often the most available in pet stores, this type of leash is reliable and durable.

Retractable Leash

For owners who prefer a bit more freedom (or lack thereof) during specific times in their walk routine, the retractable leash is their friend. At the push of a button, the leash can extend or, as the name implies, retract. This allows your dog more wiggle room if in a safe area that you want it to play in without necessarily taking them off the leash. They can also be restrained when the need arises. Caution is advised though, as retractable leashes have been known to cause injuries because of a careless owner's misuse of the device. Misuse can happen when the owner yanks or retracts the leash too quickly. This can lead to the dog choking and getting hurt.

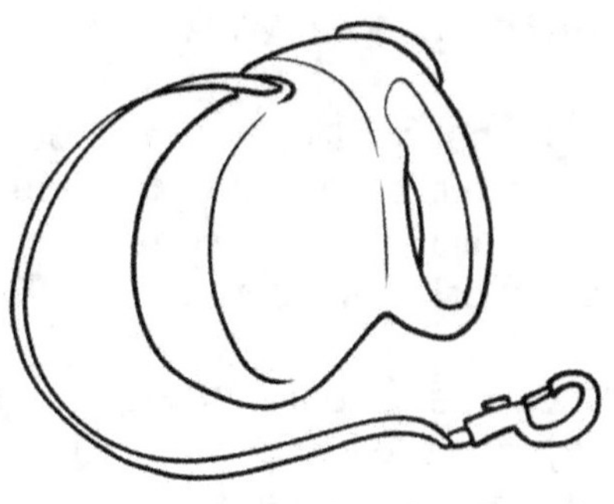

Slip Collars

A favorite of dog trainers, a slip collar (otherwise known as a choker), is a collar that can be tightened with a pull of the wrist. This is often used by professional trainers to manage or correct behaviors, but, like the retractable leash, can definitely result in injury to your dog if abused or used incorrectly. It is best to learn how to use one from an actual trainer, and not to use it as a means to punish a misbehaving dog.

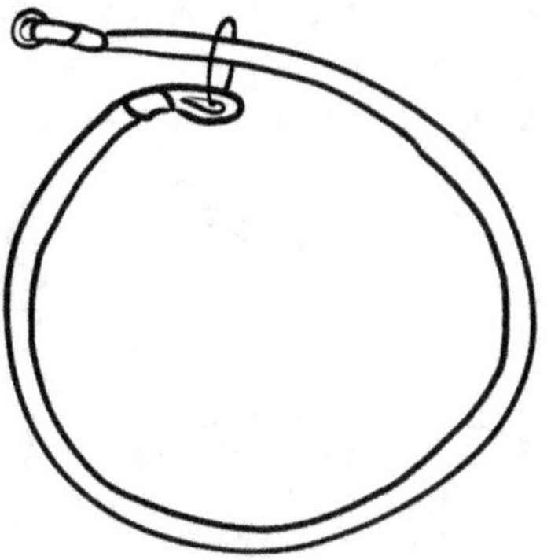

For regular dog owners, a slip collar can be handy when conventional collars are either too loose or too tight on their own. This is usually the case for bigger dogs.

Encountering Other Dogs

Chances are, there will be other dogs walking out and about with their owners in your neighborhood. It is inevitable that you'll have to interact with them. You will have to be the one to make sure that things go smoothly, and to react if anything bad happens between your dog and that of your neighbor's. Here are a few tips to follow:

1. Remain calm. If you encounter another owner with their dog on the street, avoid sudden movements. Yanking your dog away or rushing to the other side won't help as it will teach your dog that other dogs are a threat.
2. Be friendly. Greet your fellow dog owner, and allow your dog to approach their dog.
3. Observe your dog's behavior as well as your fellow owner's dog. If either of them begin to display aggressiveness such as growling or baring teeth, draw them away immediately.
4. If things are peaceful between your dog and theirs, allow the dogs to sniff each other.
5. Just like before, avoid yelling, screaming, or doing sudden movements.
6. Once the two dogs have greeted each other, calmly call to your dog and resume your walk. Reward them for good behavior with a pat or a word of praise.

Taking Responsibility

Whenever you take your dog out for a walk around your neighborhood, you have to keep in mind that you're a part of your local community as well. Other people will be walking on the same road and sidewalk you and your dog are using.

Parks, forests, and sidewalks are all public areas that you have to be considerate of. You cannot always rush home while carrying your dog when they start to poo outside. So, you must take responsibility for your dog's droppings. In fact, some communities penalize pet owners for allowing their dogs to poo in public areas and leaving the mess for others to clean up.

During walks, it's helpful to carry around a few plastic bags, and a broom and pan, or a pair of plastic gloves. Always pick up after your dog and dispose of their droppings in the proper trash bin. Remember, it's never fun to step in dog poo, so be considerate of others. After all, you wouldn't want it happening to you, right? (For more information, see page 45 on "'The Business' in The Great Outdoors")

Chapter 8
Keeping Clean

But, you might also need to wash up after.

Baths Aren't Just for People

"Oh dear," muttered Bea. "He's going in the tall grass again."

Leah leapt at Brownie and carried him away from the thick vegetation that sprawled over most of the park.

"I'm glad that he's finally eager going out," said Bea, "but he's a bit too enthusiastic about all this dirt. How are you doing?"

"I'm doing fine, Bea," answered Leah. "I can sort of control him a bit better now."

"That's good," Bea nodded approvingly.

Bea, Leah, and Brownie came home half an hour later. Leah fixed herself up while Brownie ran straight for his water bowl. They bid Bea farewell as she went on her way.

"Tomorrow after school, I want you to give Brownie a good bath," Mrs. Reyes urged. "The boy's a filthy mess!"

Bea told Leah not to ask or take advice from Nathan, but on the ride home, she couldn't help herself and prodded him.

"Well," he started. "I just chain my dog, Max, to a post and splash her down with a hose!"

"That can't be right," whispered Leah. "That sounds so mean!"

As soon as she got home, Leah pulled out her Big Book and looked over at the section on grooming.

"I knew it!" she exclaimed. "There's definitely a much better way!"

How to Bathe a Dog

A clean pup is a healthy pup. Keeping their coats clean is a step towards good hygiene for your dog and the entire house. This chapter's all about how to do it!

Identifying your dog's needs

Before we begin, we have to know what kind of dog we have and their specific needs in terms of personal hygiene. Each dog is different, not only in terms of their breed, but also their personality, health, and quirks. We first have to address the most obvious, though: their physical traits.

Dogs come in all shapes and sizes, and in this book, we'll try to tackle techniques that cover some of the most common breeds that owners usually adopt or raise.

Things of Importance

We'll start by preparing the necessary items!

1. **A Place for Giving a Bath** - We'll need a place to give our dogs a bath. Small breeds can be bathed in a sink deep enough that only their head sticks out of the countertop. Larger dogs can be bathed in a bathtub or a garage.

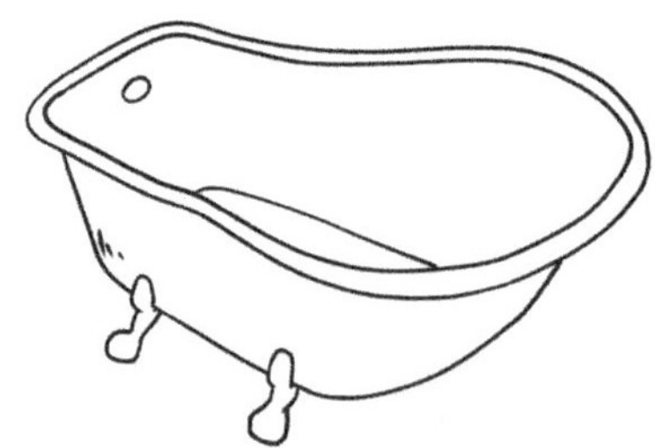

2. **Water** - We'll need to find a way to bring water to your dog. This should be easy enough if you're bathing your dog in the kitchen sink or in the bath tub. If you're outdoors and far from a hose, prepare a bucket of clean, fresh water.

3. **Shampoo** - Dogs use a different kind of shampoo from us humans. Some breeds have fur that is more delicate than others. You can ask your vet what type of shampoo is best for your dog since dog shampoos have different variants. Make sure to uncap them before the bath!

4. **Cotton balls** - Use clean cotton balls to wipe down the inside of your dog's ears before and after a bath. During bathing, you may also use a clean set to block your dog's ears to prevent too much water from entering. The ears are very sensitive as they can get infected if water enters inside. Be careful as only to set it in lightly, just enough that it does not fall out on its own.

5. **Clean towels** - Help your dog dry off by rubbing them down with a clean towel.

> **Note:**
> Some dogs with long, fluffy fur also need to be dried off with a hair dryer. Always keep the hair dryer at a distance, and use it without heat if possible.

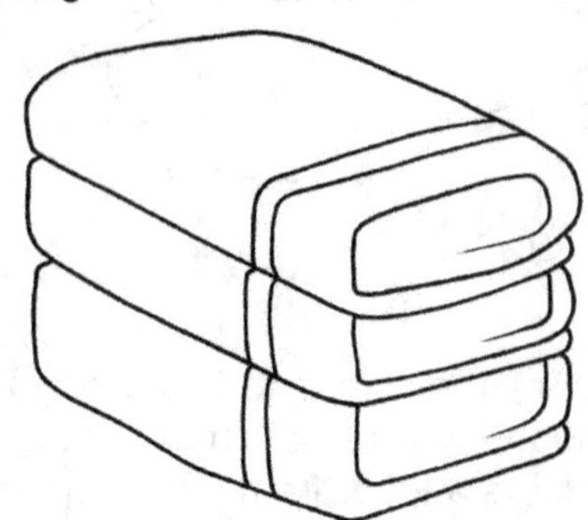

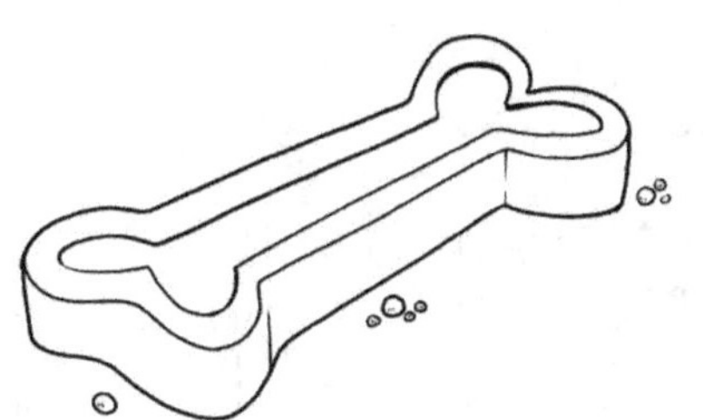

6. **Treats** - It may not come as a surprise that dogs don't like getting baths since they don't like getting wet in general. A bath is often a very terrifying experience for a dog. Help them through the bathing experience with a bit of encouragement.

> **Tip!** Keep a change of clothes for yourself! Your dog will try and shake off the water mid-bath and there's nothing you can really do but get wet, too.

Bath Time

Step 1: Guide your dog gently to where you intend to give them a bath. This may be easier with smaller dogs that you can carry, but bigger dogs will definitely need a bit of convincing.

Avoid using physical violence! Don't intentionally hurt your dog if they don't cooperate. A gentle voice, a soft pat on their rump, and loving petting can go a long way.

Step 2: Remove your dog's collar. You'll want to keep their collars off for the bath, especially if they're made of material that shrinks in water such as leather. If you cannot control your dog without a leash, try using nylon collars as they are waterproof.

Step 3: Do the first wash. Run lukewarm water over your dog's body to get it used to the sensation and to prepare its fur for the shampoo. Run the water starting from your dog's neck and then down. Remember to avoid the ears. Gently rub its wet fur. Keep praising your dog for being still to encourage that good behavior! Dogs like hearing their humans being loving and kind.

Step 4: Lather shampoo over your dog's fur. If your dog has short-hair. Pour the shampoo over your dog and rub the shampoo over its fur to lather it. Make sure you fully coat the fur from the neck down!

If your dog has long hair, it will help to pre-lather your shampoo beforehand by pouring it in a pail with some water to make a nice even coat for your dog. After creating the lathered mix, apply as normal.

Step 5: Rinse off the shampoo. Give your dog a nice splash of water to wash away the suds. Keep rubbing your dog's fur to make sure the water reaches every nook and cranny, taking care to avoid the ears. It won't be very pleasant to your dog if a bit of shampoo dries and mats their fur. When fur gets matted, it becomes a solid clump of fur that is uncomfortable for your dog.

Step 6: Clean your dog's face. You can't do the same thing you did with the rest of its body because its face is a lot more sensitive. For this, use a damp towel to wipe down their face. Again, avoid the ears. Some dogs have wrinkly faces, and a lot of dirt can get stuck in between those wrinkles! Make sure to pay extra attention to them, as any dirt left there can become infections!

Step 7: Dry-off your dog's fur. The moment you take your hands off your dog, they might realize that the bath is over, and will shake themselves vigorously to dry off. Prepare the towel, and cover yourself if you're uncomfortable getting splashed with water. Don't stray too far, though! Your dog needs to know that the bath isn't over yet! Make sure you put the towel over them quickly before they run off, and do your best to dry them off with a towel as much as you can.

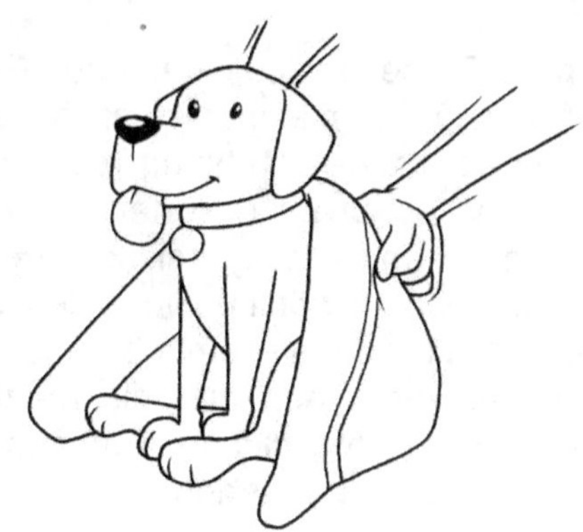

Don't worry if the dog isn't 100% dry after. They can shake and air-dry themselves well enough.

Step 8: If you have a long-haired dog, it is necessary to make sure they are 100% dry. In this case, a hair-dryer will certainly help. Make sure you keep a good distance between your dog and the hair dryer as those things can get hot! If you're not sure how to use one, consult a friend or a family member before you use it on your dog.

And, you're done! The dog is clean and fluffy and… Oh no, they're in the garden again!

Tips for Everyday Care

- Brush your dog's fur regularly. It's not necessary to bathe a dog every day, only once every two weeks. In between washings, your dog's fur may get matted and stuck. A good brushing habit will prevent that from happening.

- Train your dog to avoid areas and behaviors that might lead to getting them too dirty. Follow them around as they explore and use a command word like "no" and shoo them off.

- Keep your house clean! It's okay to have a dog get dirty after playing in the yard or the park as it can't be helped. Keeping your own house free of dirt and dust will help keep your dog clean and happy! After all, they are your pet and not a living duster.

Brushing Teeth

It is important to keep your dog's teeth clean and healthy. They use their mouth and teeth for other things, too, like grabbing things. Keep them nice and shiny with these simple steps.

1. Use a special dog toothbrush that you can buy at your vet's office or at a pet store.
2. Special dog toothpaste is also available for purchase. Avoid using human toothpaste for your dog.
3. Lift your dog's lips so as to reveal the gums and teeth.
4. Gently brush its teeth on the outside, the part facing the cheeks.
5. Avoid the tongue-facing side as it may agitate your dog.
6. Be sure to reward your dog with praise for a job well done.

Brushing the Fur

Keeping your dog's fur brushed helps keep it clear of dirt and parasites. It also contributes to keeping their coat shiny and fresh. Other than that, they just simply enjoy the whole thing!

1. Brush a long-haired dog's fur at least once a week. Short-haired dogs don't need their fur to be brushed frequently.
2. Using a special bristle-tipped brush, gently brush in the direction the coat grows. Brushing in the opposite direction ruins their coat and makes your dog uncomfortable.

Trimming Nails

In order to avoid damage to persons and objects, you have to keep your dog's nails trimmed. A regular schedule should be maintained for this.

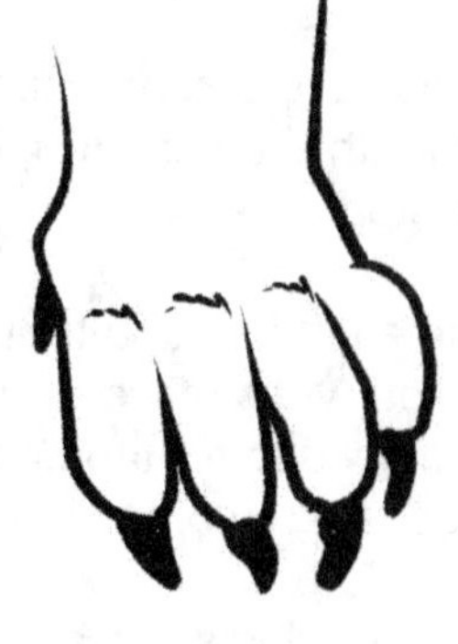

1. Prepare a specialized dog nail trimmer, as well as a styptic powder, a substance used to stop bleeding. The latter is necessary if you trim too far into what is called the quick and cause bleeding.
2. Hold your dog's paw gently and trim one nail at a time. Special trimmers often have a limiter that blocks you from pushing them too far in.
3. Nails are tough, so if you find yourself cutting something soft and spongy, you might be at the quick, which is a small portion nearer the paw that holds blood. Stop immediately.
4. If your dog gets anxious, it's alright to do the trimming one paw at a time. Break it up with a few activities like a walk or some play in between.

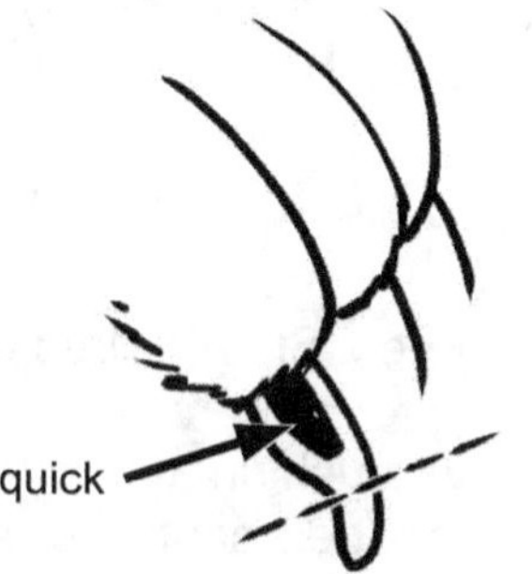

Note:
To use the styptic powder, dip the bleeding nail into it and hold for a few seconds.

Cleaning the Face

Your dog's face can be at risk of infection if not cleaned regularly. This is especially true for dogs with wrinkled faces like pugs and shar-peis.

1. Remember that the face is a sensitive area for your dog. Be gentle.
2. Use a damp cloth to wash their face. Smooth-skinned dogs such as retrievers don't need to be washed often.
3. Wrinkly-faced dogs like pugs tend to gather plenty of dirt under their folds. Take care in wiping it down. Be gentle, but firm.

Cleaning the Ears

Another place that could be at risk of infection are your dog's ears. They provide the most direct route for germs and bacteria to enter your dog's sensitive insides, so it pays to keep them regularly clean.

1. Prepare materials such as cotton balls, cleaning solution, and specialized pliers called hemostats that can be purchased anywhere that sells medical supplies, not just veterinarian clinics.
2. Avoid using cotton buds as they tend to push dirt and debris further into a dog's ears.
3. Cleaning solution can be prepared at home using one part white vinegar to one part of water.
4. Grab a cotton ball using a hemostat and dab it lightly in cleaning solution.
5. Help your dog to relax with some praise and belly rubs.
6. Work from the inside out. Rub dirt away from the inside of the ears to the outside.

Chapter 9
It's All Fun and Games
Who knew heaven was a place on Earth?

Max Goes Missing!

Leah was playing with Brownie in the living room one day when the Reyes' home was disturbed by an orchestra of mad doorbells. Mrs. Reyes answered the door and found Nathan, bruised and blubbering, asking to see Leah.

"Max ran away!" he stammered. "Brownie's got a good nose, doesn't he? You've got to help!"

"What's going on?" asked Mr. Reyes.

"I don't know!" screamed Nathan.

"Somebody at home left the front door open and the next thing I knew, Max was down the street running! I haven't seen her since. Please, you've got to help!"

Leah tutted. "Bea says it's because you're mean to your dog!" she scolded. "Maybe she finally ran away so you can't hurt her anymore!" She felt her father's hand on her shoulder, squeezing it lightly.

"Leah, now's not the time to be blaming anybody for this," said Mr. Reyes. "We don't dismiss a call for help, especially if there's something we can do about it."

"But, what can we do about it?" Leah asked.

"For starters, let the boy in," said Mrs. Reyes. "He looks like he could use some food and a bit of rest."

"And I'll call the barangay hall," blurted Mr. Reyes. "Tell them about a missing pet. Keep an eye on Nathan, will you, anak?"

Hours passed in the Reyes' household, and Leah and Nathan huddled around the telephone in the living room. Mr. and Mrs. Reyes went about their day, checking in on the two every so often to assure them that they'll find poor Max eventually.

Shortly before dinner, there was a knock on the door. It was the local tanod, and he had a small, furry friend with him. Nathan burst out of the Reyes' front door and ran towards his dog, but Max ran behind the tanod and hid there.

"Max!" Nathan screamed. "Get over here, you bad dog! You made me worry!" Max whimpered. She tried to run off but the ranger caught her by the scruff of her neck.

"It doesn't look like she wants to come back home with you," huffed the tanod.

"That's stupid!" Nathan yelled back. "Of course, she does! She just knows that she did something bad and she's ashamed!"

"She's scared of you, Nathan," quipped Leah. "She doesn't want to go with you because you're mean to her!"

Leah walked towards Max, still cowering behind the tanod's legs. She knelt down and reached out and opened her hand. Leah called out to Max with a few treats, and eventually she came to her.

"Good girl!" Leah squeaked.

"How did you do that?" muttered Nathan. "She never comes to me!"

"It's really simple!" answered Leah. "Do you want me to teach you?"

Nathan hesitated for a second before nodding his head. Leah guided Max back to him, and took his hand to put it on the dog's head.

"You have to promise to be a good owner from now on, okay?" she said.

"I promise!" replied Nathan.

Having Fun with your Dog

There are plenty of ways to have fun with your dog. The best I find is to simply spend time with them.

Dogs are precious creatures, capable of imitating and reflecting the people who surround them with a strange resemblance. Whenever we talk to them or spend our routines with them, they begin to pick up traits we normally only see in other humans. Some dogs even go so far as to imitate the sounds that their owners make, almost to a point where it's as if they almost managed to speak.

"Mishka the Talking Dog"

It is in these little nuances where we see more of ourselves in them. We begin to treat them more as we would treat ourselves (save for the diet, of course.).

Little comforts such as playing them music or just physically playing with them help us find peace and fulfillment in caring for these simple creatures as our companions.

Fun Things to Teach Your Dog

Fetch – A simple enough activity to do. Get a tennis ball, head out to the nearest park, and entice your dog with the ball. When you have them interested in the ball, throw it!

> **Tip!** If your dog refuses to give up the ball, offer him a treat while pairing it with the command, "give." Your dog will let go of the ball to grab the treat.

Music – If you play a musical instrument or you sing, it might make for a good bonding activity between you and your dog. Dogs love music, and they'll love it when they see you having fun making it.

Running – If you're more athletically-inclined, take your dog out for runs. Make sure to strap on your best running gear. Have a loose grip on your dog's leash to make sure it's comfortable keeping pace with you.

One Happy Family

It was a quiet Friday after school, and Mr. Reyes decided to leave work early to pick up Leah. He'd swung by their house beforehand and picked up Brownie, too. They drove down to the dog park, settled on a bench, and let Brownie off his leash.

After spending a few minutes frolicking in the open field by himself, Brownie returned to Leah, pawing at her feet.

"Do you want to play, boy?" she asked. Brownie barked into the air and ran circles around them. Leah reached into her bag and pulled out an old tennis ball. She showed it to Brownie, who started jumping up and down repeatedly the moment he saw his favorite toy. Leah threw it as hard as she could, and Brownie chased after it like a bolt of lightning.

Mr. Reyes had been watching Leah and Brownie from afar, when someone tapped his shoulder. It was Bea, and they both nodded their heads in greeting.

"How are they doing?" Bea asked.

"Wonderful," said Mr. Reyes. "I used to dream about having my own dog when I was a child. Seeing Leah and Brownie together having fun makes me very happy."

"Say," continued Mr. Reyes. "What are you doing here?"

As he turned, he spotted Nathan and his dog, Max, walking side by side in the distance. Max was smiling and wagging her tail, for the first time. Nathan was, for the first time as well, treating his dog like a friend. They both looked very happy.

"I have a new pair of students," chuckled Bea before she waved goodbye and left.

Mr. Reyes looked back at Leah and Brownie. They had been messing around on the grass. Leah was laughing and Brownie was licking her face. Mr. Reyes looked at them and smiled.

Bibliography

American Kennel Club. n.d. *Be A Responsible Dog Owner*. Accessed 07 29, 2017. http://www.akc.org/dog-owners/responsible-dog-ownership/.

American Society for the Prevention of Cruelty to Animals. n.d. *General Dog Care. Accessed* 07 29, 2017. https://www.aspca.org/pet-care/dog-care/general-dog-care.
—. n.d. *People Foods to Avoid Feeding Your Pets*. Accessed 07 29, 2017. https://www.aspca.org/pet-care/animal-poison-control/people-foods-avoid-feeding-your-pets.

Bender, Amy. 2017. *Top 10 Basic Dog Training Commands*. 06 04. Accessed 07 29, 2017. https://www.thespruce.com/basic-dog-training-commands-1117311.

Jenna Stregowski, RVT. 17. *10 Steps to Train Your Dog*. 09 04. Accessed 07 29, 2017. https://www.thespruce.com/steps-to-train-your-dog-1118273.

Marcelo, Gio. n.d. *Basic Obedience*. Accessed 07 29, 2017. http://k9manila.com/basic-obedience/.

PetMD. n.d. *Dog Symptom Checker*. Accessed 07 29, 2017. http://www.petmd.com/dog/dog-symptom-checker.

Royal Canin. 2014. *Down to Basics: The Grooming Essentials Every Dog Owner Needs to Know*. 07 24. Accessed 07 29, 2017. http://www.mypetreference.com/2014/07/24/The-Grooming-Essentials-Every-Dog-Owner-Needs-to-Know.

American Veterinary Medical Association. n.d. *12 Dog Diseases You Can Combat with Vaccination and Deworming*. Accessed 07 29, 2017.
https://www.avma.org/public/PetCare/Pages/dogs.aspx

Paddock, Arliss. 2016. Spaying and Neutering Your Puppy or Adult Dog: Questions and Answers. 5 26. Accessed 10 2, 2017. http://www.akc.org/content/health/articles/spaying-and-neutering-your-dog-faqs/.

PetMD. n.d. Canine Coronavirus Infection in Dogs. Accessed 10 2, 2017. http://www.petmd.com/dog/conditions/digestive/c_dg_canine_coronavirus_infection.
—. n.d. Distemper in Dogs. Accessed 10 2, 2017. http://www.petmd.com/dog/conditions/respiratory/c_dg_canine_distemper.
—. n.d. Parvo in Dogs. Accessed 10 2, 2017. http://www.petmd.com/dog/conditions/infectious-parasitic/c_dg_canine_parvovirus_infection.

Acknowledgment

My parents, for giving me a loving home and everything that comes with it. Without them, I would not have been here to write this book nor all the other works of art I have been able to accomplish. Honestly, they deserve a whole book just to acknowledge how much they've helped me, but we'll keep this one brief.

Soledad Racho, for introducing me to my publisher Kahel Press and giving me this rare opportunity to have a book published. She has been a dear friend since the day I met her and she continues to give me blessings.

Wowie Catabijan and Kahel Press, for giving me the chance to have my first children's book published. By the time this book reaches your hands, I, Wowie, and the rest of Kahel would have gone through so much to accomplish all the things we'd done, and all of us would be stronger for it.

My friends, who have given me support during my most trying times, helping me along just to get this—and all my other projects—finished in time with my sanity intact.

My mentors, who have given me guidance and taught me from experience. Without them, I would have made a lot more mistakes than I would have liked.

And finally, the Universe, for conspiring to have me do the right things and meet the right people at the right times.

About the Author

Ransom Rogers is an enigmatic fellow: a lover of dogs, games, and chicken nuggets. He is known to take life a lot less seriously than most other people, often seen stargazing at three in the afternoon by the local park. Take care when approaching Ransom, as he frightens easily. An offering of orange juice is advised. Ransom writes and draws a multitude of different things, from the comics you buy in the bookstore to the cartoons you see on the afternoon lineup. However, he uses many names and many faces for each of these, suitably to match the seriousness or the wackiness that is required to do his work. But he mostly keeps them to scare away the mole rats that keep hanging out on his favorite park bench.

www.ingramcontent.com/pod-product-compliance
Lightning Source LLC
Chambersburg PA
CBHW060120120726
48003CB00009B/2716